For Melissa,

I can't thank you
enough for seeing
this story.

Endless gratitude,

Coco Mecracken ☺

dec 2022

More Praise for *The Rabbit*

"In Coco McCracken's fantastic, punkified coming-of-age story, we get invited to the mosh pits and the smoke-filled, teenage basements and the cramped backseats of cars in search of belonging. It comes at a cost. Because in this searing memoir, a battle is being waged inside our narrator: whiteness has taken 'a hammer to the Asian girl.' McCracken's electrifying prose locates the site of the wounds—of both self-love and mother love. The book reminds us forcibly that memory can help us heal if we pin it to the page this beautifully."

–Susan Conley,
Author of *Landslide* and *Elsey Come Home*

"The beauty in *The Rabbit* is that it is so very relatable to those who have longed, loved, lost, and learned… and it is a testament to not just the universality but the multiversality of the intersectional experience. In this case, the coming-of-age experience of Coco McCracken."

—Marpheen Chann,
Author of *Moon in Full: A Modern Coming-of-Age Story*

The Rabbit

Coco McCracken

Maine Chapbook Series
Maine Writers & Publishers Alliance
2022

This is for us, the malcontents.

The fence climbers, the pool hoppers, the barn shakers, the late-night roof runners. The kids who found all that love, all that family, in those forgotten suburban basements.

Here's to us now and then, elbows out, swirling around the pit, hands to the sky.

"Sing me something soft
Sad and delicate
Or loud and out of key
Sing me anything
We're glad for what we've got
Done with what we've lost
Our whole lives laid out right in front of us."

As much as my journals and loved ones confirm the following events, much of the dialogue has been re-imagined. Except, of course, for a few searing sentences I will never be able to forget, and a thousand little details permanently etched in my being. I'll carry all of them with me until I'm stardust again.

ISBN: 978-1-7356732-4-0

©2022
Published in the United States of America
by the Maine Writers & Publishers Alliance
Portland, Maine

Publication made possible by grants from the Maine Arts Commission,
the Margaret E. Burnham Charitable Trust, and the Nichols Fund.

Cover image by Jessica Myer
Author Photo Jennifer Bravo

Book Design & Editing by Pink Eraser Press

Contents

Introduction

I see her hiding behind the camera.

Did we all have that friend in high school who brought her camera everywhere because taking pictures of everyone else gave her something to do? The camera kept her at the center of the party or the punk rock show, but it allowed her to keep a safe distance as she slipped behind it. She would tell us that she stood on the periphery for the shot or for better lighting. She couldn't be too close—for the sake of the picture. We believed her.

I had a crush on my photographer friend in high school, but I didn't know how to talk to her. How do you get close to someone who hides? How do you get to know her? Who is she? What does she like—no, *what is she like?*

Years later, I now know that my photographer friend was hiding in plain sight, right there in front of us. I thought she was inscrutable and shy, but all I had to do was look at her photographs. We were thick-headed, teenage boys, but with her camera, she made us look charismatic and fun—and important. At least, she made us *feel* important because she aimed her lens at us. Our parents took pictures only of important occasions, and there she was, taking pictures of us.

If we had taken the time to see what she saw, we would have known more about her than she could have ever told us.

This is the magic trick of *The Rabbit*.

As a photographer by trade and writer by avocation, Coco McCracken takes us through her photo album. *Here is her childhood. These are her teenage years. That's her family. This is alcoholism. This is divorce. Those people are her friends. That guy there? He is her heartthrob. He is also her heartbreak.*

The Rabbit is a story of a girl hiding behind the camera, and in telling her story, she is courageously pushing herself in front of it.

Kazuo Ishiguro, in his 2017 Nobel Prize speech, says, "But in the end, stories are about one person saying to another: This is the way it feels to me. Can you understand what I'm saying? Does it also feel this way to you?"

Like all the best storytellers and photographers, Coco McCracken is asking her own version of those questions, asking the reader to see the beauty and sadness and transcendence that she sees.

Is *The Rabbit* about hiding or is it about revelation? Do you get to know Coco McCracken or does she hide at the edges behind her camera? Whom do you see in these pages? Is this her story? Or did you catch a glimpse of yourself in there, too?

That's her magic trick.

—Phuc Tran

The

Rabbit

Battle Royale

"Wait, all we need is glue and a hair dryer?"

"Yeah, Elmer's works fine. Maybe put an extra layer on for tonight."

Somehow, I've been granted the honor of setting Copeland's mohawk before the show. Taking a sip of the lukewarm Labatt 50, I try not to grimace as the flat beer rolls down my throat. I worry that blow drying his hair in this tiny bathroom will enhance the flush of my cheeks and upper chest. My mom jokes that my Irish blood craves the alcohol that simultaneously poisons my sensitive Chinese cells, and I am determined to have the two countries conduct a battle-royale inside me until a winner is declared.

It's only been a semester since I met "the guys," thanks to Comms & Tech, a class I take with Jeff. "Tech" is being generous, since we're learning how to edit film using JVC terminals from the 80s, which look like supercomputers beneath teeny 10-inch monitors. To stitch scenes together, we literally cut and paste acetate. Plugging in the red, yellow, and white cords to provide the audio and video for our projects is as close as I ever get to feeling like a magician — other than hanging out with this new motley crew of castaways.

Even though he lives 450 meters from my front door, I had never really met Jeff before my junior year of high school. It probably had something to do with the fact that he sat in class next to Sully, my heart-obliterating, pen-chewing, journal-scribbling crush. If crushes at that age block one's peripheral vision, being enamored with Sully was like happily putting on horse-blinders every morning, and then trotting in slow circles from the first to last school bell.

In just one semester, my best friend Lex and I have gone from watching *The OC* and *Survivor* in her basement while pining over celebrity crushes, to experimenting with eardrum-shattering activities that involved real-life male specimens. Jeff, Sully, and their friends are in a band that I assume don't sound like anything I've ever heard, because they don't dress or act like any people I've ever met.

I can't believe just plain-white glue, the kind kids use to make flimsy popsicle houses, is responsible for this eyebrow-raising updo that sends most parents to the other side of the mall when they spot us. Fresh out of the shower, Copeland lets me dry his hair into a floppy black mass, and thick little waves create soft side bangs that frame his green eyes. I ready the glue while I check my makeup. He doesn't need to wear eyeliner like I do; his Italian eyelash follicles naturally frame his lids. He tells me to start. I'm beet red, and tiny hives are emerging along my collarbone, but I grab another beer from the fridge. This time I'll drink it quickly.

The Cardinal

Just a year prior, I was floundering in high school between tepid friendships. Having lost a group of best friends in eighth grade, I entered the ninth with supremely low self-esteem. For the first half of my time at Brother Andre Catholic High, I took what I could get, in every possible sense.

Friends evolved from group projects. If other kids perused a menu, wondering which human was best suited to their tastes, I never asked to see it. I waited for them to order first and followed with, "I'll just have the same." By not stepping on the toes of my peers, I rooted myself as the quiet, well-oiled wheel. I never named it then, my feeling of worthlessness. A part of me knew that accepting it might crush me in more terminal, devastating ways. My survival strategy was to ignore the feeling as best as I could and circle back to myself as an adult, when I hoped I'd be stronger.

My high school heart was devoted to lighting up gardenia-scented candles while I brushed up on my Elvish and wrote fan mail to Elijah Wood. I didn't think my taste in celebrities was eccentric then, but my peers enjoyed reminding me. Watching *The Faculty*, I let the girls at sleepovers breathily sigh over every Josh Hartnett scene, while I felt grateful for the space around Elijah to entertain my fantasies. I needed to set any bar, including my celebrity crush, within grasp. With hobbies like mine, I could safely cordon off any potential of being part of the popular crowd. I couldn't risk bringing new friends home, anyway. What if we walked into my room right when the sun hit my life-size poster of Frodo Baggins, his open mouth shining under a thick layer of Lip Smacker?

I did fall for the beauty traps. I was inundated with countless magazines that never reflected my face but hinted that I could get close to others *with the right tricks!* There usually was at least one Asian model in the final editorial, wearing "electric yellow" eyeshadow and hair cut in a razor-edged bob. Always the sporty look, and always relegated to the back pages. Thanks to endless amounts of fantasy novels and my preference for video games over team sports, my ideal self was more of a lithe, romantic damsel than an athlete. *Seventeen* magazine told me that to exude romance, I should touch my décolletage when a crush looked my way. This was a surefire strategy to appear demure, sexy, and confident, without being slutty. *Seventeen* also noted (in almost every issue) that beach waves were the best waves because they added a whimsical, effortless look. The ideal was tousled hair that looked as if it were fresh from riding a stallion at sunset. And for an easy-breezy, two-for-one, "on-the-go" look, I should use an eyebrow pencil to shade my eyelids. Whatever I do, though, I should *not* try too hard. Beauty was supposed to come easy.

I wonder if any of the beauty editors of the late 90s had ever met a teen girl. It would take a lot more than a swipe of eye shadow and sticking my head out of the car while driving to add beauty to my look. Unless of course, we were driving fast enough for my headgear to rip from my face. Still, I spent countless nights with pins and rollers pressed against my skull. I blow-dried my eyelash curler before pressing the hot metal to my eyes to get an hour of doe-eye. I made sure to walk past all my crushes before third period because, without fail, my slick, black hair always fell limp by lunch. No amount of smokey shadow could lift my eyes from the foxholes they were set in.

I eventually gave in and joined the athletic council, mainly because my A average needed some school-run activities to boost my college applications. Even then, my slouched shoulders gave me away before I could sneak into the VIP section, where the kids of easy youth lounged.

(For context, I had been one of only two girls who tried out for two spots on the tennis team — and they only took the other girl.) During one council meeting, the school's bright red cardinal mascot costume somehow ended up on my lap. After two soul-crushing pep rallies, this costume became a reminder of the demise of my exhausting, extracurricular climb up the ladder of high school acceptability.

While the "Spirit Squad" pom-pommed each athlete as they jogged in under erratic spotlights and Good Charlotte's "Anthem," I high-kicked and clucked my way to maniacal laughter inside the cardinal costume. My cackling only grew stronger as I watched our school's beloved and handsome hockey pros mouth the words to Joel Madden, singing, *"Another loser anthem!"* I pictured the music video of a "misfit" band that plays in an empty Malibu pool filled with rail-thin blondes, riding around on thousand-dollar BMX bikes. I shimmied myself across the basketball court floor, swirling around each cliché, bathing in the ridiculousness of it all. "Cardinals don't cluck!" came flying at me from the bleachers. I pulled my arms inside the sauna of my polyester bird body and gave the entire school the finger. It didn't matter that only I could see my bird-flipping moment. It was enough to pull the red, woolly feathers from my eyes.

After the mortifying pep rallies, I started to dig around for any signs of life hiding underneath the bleachers. Who were the kids who avoided the pep rallies — were they lazy stoners, or were they up to something more interesting than dress rehearsal cheering? The answer, of course, was sitting in front of me in Comms & Tech. Thanks to my quick stint as the high school laughingstock, I wasn't intimidated to talk to Jeff or the guys anymore. The sole exception: Sully. He could still freeze me in my tracks with one glance. His face was always warm and faintly flushed, like he had just jogged to class. But he was cold to me. Even in our eventual friendship, Sully saved lengthy opinions for his bandmates and whichever girl he was dating at the time. In all our years of knowing one another, our conversations wouldn't fill a single typed page. But still, I savored any small word he spoke to me, nibbling off them for weeks, like a lost and starving hiker pretending her last blueberry was a porterhouse.

I began to molt from an awkward mascot into a mohawk expert. And like other transformations in the natural world, before clipping on a hardened shell, I was vulnerable larvae. While Lex talked about getting a face-piercing for her birthday, I looked around my bedroom and still saw the leftover markings of a role-playing gamer. She was evolving faster than I was, but I was coming up behind her. It wasn't just the potential of a lip ring or thick-rimmed eyelids that thrilled me. It wasn't just the faint sniff of a cologned arm around my neck at the movies. There was something else that made me rip the skin from my muscle in haste, and that something had everything to do with my mother.

Carton of Cigs

Once I turned sixteen, I gave in to the pressures of my mother. I had almost made it through high school without getting drunk, smoking cigarettes, or even trying pot. But now, if I came home tired from a friend's house, she'd *wink, wink, nudge, nudge* me when I said I was "really sober, I swear!" She was a cool mom after all. With each offering of a sneaky six-pack, I can only assume she wanted to indulge her straight-talking, expletive-filled persona with a daughter who shared her likeness. Our faces never would mirror one another, though, at least not to the untrained eye. For her, the next best thing was having her eldest teen girl let loose once in a while.

For me, caving in was less about my mom and more about the raging hormones responsible for the defaced Elijah Wood poster. I was about to enter my senior year with zero history of having a boyfriend, kissing a single person, or breaking any rules. I considered my lack of rebelliousness to be directly related to my lack of French kissing experience. So, when Mom gifted me a carton of cigarettes for my half-birthday one day after school, I finally shelved the "no thank yous" and accepted the jumbo package.

It had only been a few months since meeting the guys, and, other than learning to style two-foot spikes I didn't have much to offer the group. My taste in music was horrible, and after years of being nick-named Bok Choy, I was only holding out hope that the dues from my late-blooming body would pay up soon. The landscape of my bone structure was akin to planks of wood, from my forehead to my chest, right down to my ass. If my body was a hiking trail, I would have a total elevation gain of nil. But even if I had been curvy, being "hot" wasn't enough anymore, especially not with this group of musically inclined, Orwellian teens. I needed a music library overhaul, an education in gonzo journalism, and a never-giving-a-shit attitude. I couldn't show up to my new neighborhood with a charcuterie basket. I needed to stuff it full of roman candles and light those fuckers on fire.

The red pack was small in Mom's hands, and I didn't notice any yellowed fingertips as she passed the box to me. I flicked the thin cardboard lid open and slid up the aluminum sheet, which revealed the little row of smokes. It was truly a beautiful design if I blurred my eyes over the graphic photos of oral cancer on the carton cover. No millimeter of space was wasted, and the scent of the filters, paper, and tobacco wafted together in such harmony that I could understand the urge to inhale the smoke deeply into my lungs.

Mom busied herself in the kitchen while I lit the first of the 200 cigarettes. I sensed pride in my mom as she eyed my new ritual. As I brought our footlong barbeque lighter to my face, she turned to look at me with an expression that I imagine a parent might have when seeing their child descend a staircase on prom night.

For the first time in a long time, I felt close to her again. We were now a mother-daughter duo who shared cigarettes. Maybe we'd move to wine next. I wondered if this was how it felt to be an adult, knowing that after I stubbed out the cigarette filter in the ashtray, an endless supply awaited me in my backpack. For all the stumbling and falling I had achieved in high school, I was now a smoker who would never have to mooch off friends during parties. I strutted confidently into the direction ahead, hoping that my first love wouldn't be too far behind.

Baby's First Mosh Pit

"The lips shirt is my favorite," I tell Lex. She's looking through her closet for the fifth time, something I've never seen her do. A pair of illustrated red lips plaster the center of a black, off-the-shoulder dress. The mouth resembles hers, and when she sees herself in the mirror, her upper right canine bites her lower right lip in the same sultry, slightly confused, come-hither kind of way. I'm in another mirror, globbing on as much eyeliner as possible without coloring my corneas black.

"Yeah, it's my hair, though. It's just so boring," she tells me. Her silky brown hair is shimmering and freshly blow-dried. It catches light at the edge of her chest, where her locks cascade into a romantic swing, ending at her hip bones. Rapunzel had nothing on Lex's hair. We do the usual exchange that goes a little something like this:

"Ugh, I'd give anything for your hair."

"Ugh, but *your* hair is so thick, *so* lush."

"Ew, no one wants thick. It's coarse and gross."

"Yeah, but mine is fine and limp."

"Yours can hold a curl, though."

Eventually, the cycle of compliments and self-deprecation sputters out, and the winner is revealed. The winner accepts their victory by offering condolences to the "loser" with a remedy, usually a beauty product. The recommendation is half-assed because it's just an excuse to end the relentless, useless, but engrained conversation that so many teen girls are taught to endure.

"I think I saw this new product that makes even coarse hair soft and beach wavy. You should try it," Lex says.

My hair is always the most stubborn in a group of girls. In my youth, I was constantly surrounded by brunettes and blondes who had more "agreeable locks" for tools like crimpers and curling irons. My hair was dubbed the bullheaded aunt: too opinionated, never budging. As if standing in protest to assimilation, Chinese hair is almost impervious to curls or hair dye. Chinese malls in the 90s were filled with fancy salons that charged hundreds of dollars to strip hair of any black coloration before the customer chose a new neon hue inspired by the latest animé (white-blonde always being the most popular, the most unattainable). Perms were a popular way for Asian teens of any gender to score that romantic look that all the perfume ads propagated at the time. While fair-haired friends promised that a combination of sunshine and lemons would brighten my hair, I knew that to get anywhere close to orange, I'd have to spend a day soaked in hydrogen peroxide.

Some malls even had surgeon's offices tucked in the back that offered more extreme procedures like double-eyelid surgery. I always said it was ridiculous to cut away a slice of eyelid to feel more beautiful. But a Japanese friend of mine from elementary school pointed out that, because I did have a double eyelid, I'd never understand. I judged the concept of it for years while I sizzled my scalp under chemicals and acids.

I already own the brand Lex is referring to, and I now pictured the Australian surfer girl beaming at me from my medicine cabinet. Most of the ingredients are aloe, lemon, salt, and marigold, which I know will do shit-all to my stubborn hair. Still, I'll buy another bottle with my next paycheck. Doubling up on the dosage might do the trick.

I pull up the white, blue, and red elastic band from the boy's boxer-briefs I'm wearing under my corduroy pants. Sully uttered "cool pants" in my direction this week, so it makes sense to wear the cords again. Even though we were a band of misfits, and our pierced lips and noses sectioned us apart from the "normie" cliques, we had our own set of coded approvals. We could rage against the Catholic machine that educated us all day, but I wondered if the guys would keep me into their fold if I became a star tennis player. Good thing varsity sports weren't in my future.

I tuck my Minolta SRT-101 in my backpack for extra armor. The camera was a gift from my father, and I often bring it with me to situations that make me uncomfortable so I can hide behind it. If I take photos of the guys' band, I felt permitted to be around them. An exchange of services for friendship. Really, though, my camera acts as a tool for self-gain; if I can't have Sully, I can at least have a photograph of him.

Lex and I show up at the barn, and there's already a band playing. A pirate flag covers a stained- glass window. Sounds shriek from guitars, and a boy's voice is growling in low tones, as if Metallica was at a spoken-word slam. I resist the urge to cover my ears. The music is distorted, and the drums are repetitive cymbal crashes. I wonder if I can keep up the facade of my new identity, listening to this "rock" music with a fake smile staple-gunned into my cheeks.

As a kid, when Mom was blowing our speakers to Madonna's *Ray of Light*, my move was to walk in an obvious line of her sight with hands over my ears and shoot her dirty looks. "Mom! Please! I've got homework!" I would yell once my pantomime proved useless. "I've got one life to live, Courtney! Don't be so *BO-RING*," she would shout back, making sure to elongate the second syllable for as long as possible. She never turned the volume down as she danced from one room to the next, seeming impossibly beautiful and sad at the same time.

"Boring," the enemy of every rebellious teen. Growing up in manicured suburbia, your eyes are assaulted by boring. Boring is the flavor of Kool-Aid that the popular kids drink. Bleachers are boring, football games are boring. I never want to be boring. I release the tension from my shoulders with a counterclockwise roll and tilt my head to the band. A bottle of Smirnoff Apple vodka is being passed around, and when it comes to me I take a swig. A sweet and rancid cider-like taste greets my lips, and a cinnamon burn coats my throat on the way down. The music melts into something more viscous after the chug. I still hate it, but I try to make the experience a game. Searching for some sort of rhythm in the haphazard noises, I feel a lock of heavy hair fall from a bobby pin's pathetic grasp.

Copeland and his friends, Marley and Findlay, are already in the center of the mosh pit. Copeland raises his arms up, as if to block a karate-chop. His knees follow while he releases little kicks. The other foot bounces while he adds a head-banging figure eight. It's epileptic in form, and yet each move connects so fluidly to the next. A punk rock marionette lifted by some invisible force. I look up for strings. I take another slug of the apple vodka and start to bounce on the pads of my feet. Lex has her arms crossed against her body, her lips matching the shirt again. With our eyebrows raised, we eye a joint being passed around.

Lex takes the joint without pause. She tokes a tiny inhale and returns a tinier cough. She evokes elegance, but I can tell she's just as nervous as I am. We feel eyes upon eyes from every corner of the barn. Not knowing in the slightest what being high could do to my brain, I take a drag too.

Coughing, I try to revert to my best wallflower stance. Standing as close to the edge of the room as possible, I feel every ounce of my body pull toward the swirling mosh pit. Luckily the band finishes before I'm pulled in.

"Smoke?" I ask Copeland, who's emerging from the pit, a smile as wide as his hair. I start to feel dizzy.

"Hell, yes. Also, you're coming in there with me next time."

I laugh him off and we head outside. It's just about eight, and the fresh interlude of air steadies me. A few clumps of kids exit with us and light up, shifting from Vans to Vans. We all nod at one another in this club within the club. The sunset washes everything in gold. I light up two cigarettes at once and give one to Copeland. This small practice, which I've seen in so many movies before, makes me feel powerful. Knowing I'm not attracted to Copeland adds to the armor of my new persona. I could feel my body turning on this year, waking from some sort of mechanical slumber.

Each time Sully walked with me to class, or Jeff laughed at a joke I made, I could feel the sizzles of tiny sparks fusing a new panel inside me. It was like I found a new secret level, hiding behind a moss-covered door in the strange video game that was my life. This one was less pixelated, full of kaleidoscopic colors. But there was another layer to this world, one of control. I finally felt like I could reach inside myself, grasp onto the mess of wires inside me that was short-circuiting, and plug them into the right places. Red, white, and yellow. There was something thrilling about finally having a guy's number in my phone that didn't send me into a spiral every time I dialed it. Having male friends felt really fucking cool.

"Tell me, like, how do I even do that?"

"Get in a mosh pit?"

"Yeah, like, entering seems like the most dangerous part."

"It is. But then once you're in, you're in. And don't worry if you fall. Everyone makes sure they get you up before they keep dancing."

"Dancing?" I laugh. "You call that dancing?"

"Fuck, yeah. This is music, isn't it? Don't you like it?"

"I love it." I turn the cigarette around and pinch the last drag between taut lips. I flick the filter into the dirt beneath us. "I fucking love it." Walking back inside, I see the pirate flag aglow. The sun's setting rays are hitting the stained glass, bathing Sully, Jeff, and their bandmates Pat and Dave in their glow. The nicotine sends my skin into a flurry of pins and needles. Luckily, a hypnotic ritual is being performed in front of me, and I'm anchored by focus. Slick black tubes look like a mess of eels at their feet, but one by one, they find their place in the mic stands and amps. Before my eyes, a pile of electronic junk transforms into a gleaming stage. Tamed into neat spirals, cords circle beneath the band, whose faces reflect more pop icon than teen boy.

Anticipation from the crowd chokes us into a tighter circle, and we surround the four musicians. I had known that music was an option outside of athletics or art, but not in this form. I had only been to arena concerts before tonight, huge events where you could barely see the performer, let alone the soles of their sneakers. This moment feels immersive, like a performance art piece that the audience was a crucial part of. I am sweating, nervous to be so close to the band. But with one lift of my own piece of gear, the camera shields me.

The guys are concentrating, but they are acutely aware of their surroundings. Someone yells, "FUCK YOU, DAVE! I FUCKING LOVE YOU!" Dave flashes his bright white teeth without looking up and returns, "I fucking love you too, Copeland."

I think of the pep rallies and the cheering I loathe. What makes tonight so different? Scanning the room, I see kids from all over town and different school districts. I see kids who live in government housing, plus some whose families own second houses in lake country. There are kids of all colors, but we're all de-saturated in black corduroy and tight denim. Studs detail the edges of pants and hoodies. Our hair stands vertical, or is ironed flat, two or three-toned. We look so different from the pep rally crowd, but we're just as anxious to explode, shout and release anything from our inflammable insides. What has pulled me here instead, so mightily, like my body is made from a magnet, and beneath this barn is the earth's iron core?

"God, I'm high. Can you feel your spine?" Lex holds her crossed arms tighter against her lips shirt, smothering its erotic mouth shut.

"Check, check," Pat, the lead singer and Sully's brother, bellows into the mic. The noise echoes across the barnyard, and I feel so out-of-place and so at-home at the same time.

I've been trying to avoid Sully all night, but I see him now, tuning his bass. Each of the beads on his wooden necklace reflects an earth-toned hue pulled from his outfit: an off-white collared shirt, a mossy green tie, navy Dickies, and walnut hair. He flicks his head back every odd second, attempting to make his locks stick, but they never do.

Each time he scans the room, I notice him pausing longer on me. As every magazine has taught me, I try to remain expressionless. I reach for my collarbone where red welts from the vodka are appearing. How can I do what Copeland did but also exude my inner Aussie-surfer? I press my fingers hard against my scalp, lifting upward, trying to inject some body into my hair. I look around for any other girls, but it's just me and Lex at the edge of the pit. I picture the girls from our school here, dancing in tube tops the way they do at music video parties, grinding with their hands in the air. I imagine them being swallowed by a ravenous mosh pit. Getting crushed by Doc Martens. I smile. I'm definitely high.

For two full seconds, there is absolute quiet. We hold our breath.

"One, two — one-two-three-four!"

With one swift movement, Jeff's hands soar to the ceiling, a drumstick in each palm. His mouth hangs wide open, and he crashes his arms into the cymbals with precise power. I am electrocuted in the moment, the fog of the Smirnoff on pause. Sully leans forward and backward in the rigid, ship-like way bass players do. Pat is singing, and Dave is playing guitar, and the mosh pit is swirling again. It takes less than a few seconds for Copeland's hands to reach for mine. I look back at Lex. She seems whiter than usual and shakes her head no, vigorously.

"You got this!" Copeland shouts. He doesn't wait for a reply. He grabs my hand and leads me into what I can only describe as a comic strip fight, 'kapow!' and stars outlining its circumference. I somehow lock eyes with some of the other guys, and they take a second from the seriousness of this dance to smile at me. *We've got you! 'Bows out! Keep them high! Block your face!* Instructions come from Copeland, Marley, and some other guys I haven't met yet.

There are so many iterations of this experience in folklore: a secret world that exists beneath a push of a wardrobe, inside a medicine bag, after a concussion. Snow-dusted pines part way to Narnia, Merlin's bag reveals an entire house, the yellow brick road unfurls in technicolor. From the outside, this mosh pit is chaos. It's dangerous and unsavory. From the inside, I see spooling cogs and have an urge to throw wrenches into them. Pat projects a song across the room while I duck my head under the elbows of these strangers. Even if Sully sees me, there are too many limbs flailing, too many erratic movements, to stop and worry about how I look. Everyone is *busy*.

In the course of my small life, I have never seen anything like this. Who taught us that 'dancing' meant hands straight out touching shoulders, hips convex and bending backward, bodies averting magnetic pulses, eyes avoiding contact. You have to have eye contact in a mosh pit if you want to survive. Eye contact tells the other person you're paying attention. It might seem like punches are being thrown, but none are landing on purpose. This is a full-body expression from a group of kids who, in large part, don't express themselves in conventional manners. So, we mosh instead. I don't know the lyrics, but my mouth is open and I'm screaming like a kid on a rollercoaster. My arms forget what to do, and for a second an elbow from stage right clips me on my chin.

"Fuck, I'm so sorry! You okay?!" a handsome boy asks while searching my face for wounds. I nod enthusiastically. I had barely felt it, thanks to the apple vodka. I push him back hard in the chest, and he laughs and pushes me back gently. Everything inside me lights on fire. My arms swing back, and my elbows get cut with the teeth of kids I've never seen before. How have I never seen them before? They've been here all along, hiding underneath the waterline, like mussels. Razor-thin shells, hair to the sky, and studded belts that might nick you if you get too close. My patience eventually shows me an opening where their innards lay bare. Soft, pearlescent orbs. Pure, innocent flesh that's so vulnerable, so easily pierced.

I grab Copeland's wrists and sling him across the pit. I am shocked at how naturally it all comes to me. "Yeaaaaasssss!" he shouts from across the room, happy to be thrown. He's already a smaller guy, but now he's a little kid. We're all little kids. We're sipping on our parents' rejected sherry, gin, and vodka — a teen tea party. We're costumed in the patchwork of our own making, scraps left behind from letter jackets and kilts. We're angry, we're happy, we're depressed, we're drunk, we're high, we're screaming, we're together. We're all here, playing at the golden hour in a beautiful barn on the side of the road no one visits anymore.

Princess Diana

By nine, I was well aware that beautiful people were cursed. By the time I turned eleven, Princess Diana's death cemented that. Still, I longed to be a part of that world of beauty. I coveted a place on the spectrum of stunning, as if I had a choice. I wanted to be more than "just pretty," but I knew that "exceptionally gorgeous" was dangerous. The heroes and heroines with staggering beauty also had the biggest targets on their backs: Snow White, Helen of Troy, Sleeping Beauty, and The Beast before the spell was cast. It seemed that the closer you stood to plain-Jane status, the less threat you posed to yourself, and the more invisible you were to everyone else.

For years, this reasoning justified the creeping ugliness that I noticed every time I finished reading *YM* magazine. When I stared at my caterpillar eyebrows, they stood up straight, taunting me with their rootedness. The gaps between my front teeth made way for a lisp that I have to this day. The gum line that was more visible on the right side of my mouth taunted onlookers with its bare pink flesh. For perfect punctuation, a faint mustache shadowed my upper lip. Replaced with the mopey face of a pre-teen, it was plain as day that all my cuteness had evaporated by then.

My first memory of coveting another woman's appearance was watching Sleeping Beauty. With flaxen hair that ended in nautilus loops, dainty feet, and a waist-trimming black corset, I trembled with envy at the opening credits. Princess Aurora didn't even have toes, for crying out loud. Mine were already spindly and long, which halted all sandal-wearing between the ages of eleven and twenty. I tried to prance through our backyard as she frolicked, but the idea of being noticed stopped me before the second skip. Trying to sing "Once Upon a Dream" in the mirror, I was aghast at how distorted my voice sounded in comparison to the operatic sounds I was so used to in the film. If only I knew that Princess Aurora was voiced by an actual opera singer, Mary Costa, I might have reeled back my expectations slightly. But instead, I charged forward with the expectation that most poor girls who lived alone in the forest without formal training, a job, or a social life could have a set of pipes *and* score the love of a real-life prince.

In 1937, Snow White became the first Disney film to steal the hearts of kids around the world. *Sixty-one years later* the first Asian princess, Mulan, hit the theaters. I tried to hide my excitement as a pre-teen, knowing I was too old for Disney cartoons, but I was there on opening day. It wasn't that I was ready for my face to be represented and canonized in princess pop culture, but I was genuinely curious how I might be depicted as a gorgeous heroine. To my crushing disappointment, Mulan decidedly went against every notion of a beautiful damsel in distress. She rejected Chinese conventional beauty by taking the path of a warrior instead. She spent the entire movie fighting as a man, in chain mail, looking more like my brother than any princess I admired. I hated Mulan.

I could tell my mom tried to thwart me from the traps of Disney Princess syndrome. Or any classically "useless" female character for that matter. Her distaste for musicals was so palpable that I wouldn't watch *The Sound of Music*, *West Side Story*, or even *It's a Wonderful Life* until my thirties. (The latter isn't a musical, but my mom also threw the Christmas feel-good movie into the pile labeled "horseshit.") Even now, though I like each of these films for their artistic merit, gripping stories, or fantastical dance numbers, I can't shake my mom's voice in the back of my head calling them all a bunch of garbage.

"Just when you're getting to the good part, this idiot starts singing a fucking show tune. Good God." Mom's sentences were cut short by her own laughter. Her guffaws started in her belly, giving them power and volume, but they got pinched as they came out through her slender nose. She was a snorter. Her unbridled laugh was so contagious that Kyle, Dakota, and I followed suit until we cried. Sometimes the four of us laughing together was almost uncontrollable, a syrupy cacophony of happiness making up for lost time.

"Uh oh," she continued. "Here comes this bitch again." The bitch was sweet Julie Andrews, floating softly down via parasol as Mary Poppins. The contrast of Mom's mock singing "A Spoonful of Sugar" to a room of three child hecklers was enough to make us laugh until we couldn't breathe. Between sips of air, we'd squeak, "Stop. Mom! I'm going to die!" We reveled in being so close to her at those moments, making fun of all the sweetness in the world, laughing as deeply and darkly as the cynics who we would become as adults.

That's not to say Mom didn't have her own altar of heroines. Judy Garland, Lucille Ball, and Princess Diana were class acts to her, even though they were what she called anyone who she saw take a sip of wine: "a bunch of drunks."

No matter how much time I spent with Mom, some of her sentences slapped me across the face with their uncensored subject matter, or straight-out grotesque references. I could say a simple, "Those shoes are so pretty, Mom!" To which she'd reply, "Those are 'come fuck me' shoes." Most nine-year-olds in the docile suburban setting of the 90s would not have understood her reference, but I knew exactly what she meant.

Around the same age, she told me that Judy Garland died sitting on the toilet. "She shit out all of her insides because she took too many drugs." Before Mom expelled that line from her mouth, we'd been chatting about Hollywood and what it might take to become an actress. Talking to my mom was like swirling, dancing and sliding across wooden floors, only to catch your heel into a deep sliver of loose oak. This detail about Judy Garland, no matter how many times she repeated it over the years, made me feel sick. Every time I went to the bathroom, I prayed to God that my insides wouldn't fall out because I took Flintstone's vitamins that morning. I never watched the *Wizard of Oz* again after I found out how the real Dorothy died. Another musical bit the dust.

Princess Di, Lucille Ball, Judy Garland — bold, funny, beautiful women who shared my mother's penchant for cropped locks and rebellion. They didn't dance in forests waiting to be kissed by some Prince Charming. Diana was a modern mother figure who tried to bring the throne into the twenty-first century. Ball was the first woman to run a major television studio while she battled patriarchal Hollywood. Garland might have been a victim of the same starlet machine, but she pushed forward, causing shit for decades while drugs and alcohol steered her ship. These women represented a real-life embodiment of Mom's favorite motto: "Life's a bitch. Then you die."

The September afternoon that Princess Diana was buried, my mom consumed every inch of our TV screen. She watched the entire service start to finish, which is saying a lot since her attention span usually was outperformed by five-year-old Dakota. Later, for Christmas, Mom would ask for Diana's biography. This request was equally remarkable because I can count on one hand how many books I ever saw Mom read in my life.

When the Princess's coffin came down the Westminster Abbey aisle, the cameras zoomed in on *MUMMY,* underlined in the center of an envelope by a child with excellent penmanship. Seeing this letter wedged in a bed of roses, backlit by hundreds of white lilies, made my heart climb into my throat. Losing my mom was my biggest fear in life. For a moment, I wondered what was written inside *MUMMY,* but then I realized that Princess Diana would never know. A dark shadow crept into my body. The eulogy, the service, the letters, the thousands of roses wrapped in plastic at the gates of Buckingham would never be seen or smelled by Princess Di. It was a terrible offense, in my mind, for her young sons to be so ignorant to write such a hopeful thing.

I looked up at my mom with a weak smile, worried I seemed too depressed to be around her. But she was so transfixed, she didn't notice me. Instead she reached for a cigarette and lit it, only taking her eyes off the TV to make sure the tobacco ignited.

"What a way to go," she murmured to no one in particular. I searched her eyes for the same sadness I was sure I had in mine, but I saw something else instead. I saw admiration.

Around that time, we were out for ice cream with our older cousins — my mom's favorite crowd. Teens were exciting to her because she could use them to test out her R-rated material, but still return them to their owners before bedtime. My cousin Jamie asked if she wanted some of his vanilla ice cream cone, which was melting fast. She grabbed it and put the whole thing in her mouth and pulled it out again. She raised her eyebrows, looked at my older cousins and me, and said, "Oh, that reminds me of something else I'm good at."

They all laughed. Someone said how "radical" she was.

"My mom would never say something like that."

"Your mom is a legend!"

My mom beamed ear to ear, skipping across the boardwalk in her raincoat, gold hoops, and layered shag bob. She could have been a Hollywood starlet in another life. A part of me felt a prick of pride that she was so remarkably different. Looking at the vanilla cone in my hands, I felt too repulsed to finish it, so I tossed it in the trashcan when no one was watching me.

A week before this, Mom picked me up from the home of a friend I had just met. This new friend, Emer, was the school bully, and I was determined to get more protection at recess. Emer's mom was not around much, so her uncle was watching us. After dinner, when Mom came to pick me up, her svelte frame lit up the storm door. In a

Chanel suit and full makeup, I wondered if she was mocking Emer's faux wood-paneled single wide with her wardrobe.

Emer's uncle was younger than she was, but he was still old enough to have salt-colored hair and the type of breath that smelled of discount beer. He and my mom hit it off immediately, and soon bottles were uncorked. While Emer and I tried to make up more games to play, we were bored with one another. Our playdate had exceeded our day at school, and it was almost midnight. Dragging our dirty socks to the living room, we were met by Mom's legs wrapped around the lap of Emer's uncle. I finally got the guts to ask to go home *for serious* this time. They stared up at us as if they were surprised children were in the house. Emer's uncle said we'd better go and kissed my mom goodbye on the cheek.

"You call that a kiss? Who am I, Snow White?" Mom leaned into him, and their tongues met before their mouths. My ears rang, but I couldn't look away from their locked faces. I closed my eyes, and all I could see was my dad's face on Christmas morning: he was blearily pouring Bailey's and coffee for Mom while we were opening stockings. Not wanting to ruin my favorite holiday with this image, I opened my eyes to see Emer's face harden into the mask that she wore before she punched a kid. She didn't hit me, but we never hung out again after that night.

I blacked out during the crying fit that I performed when Mom pushed her limits with me. The fog lifted for a moment in her white convertible which she managed to drive. "What about the beer you drank? I don't want to die," I sobbed in the front seat.

"Relachsss, it's only five minuhtss, straight shoughtt home. Die? Death? Su-chh ah drama queen."

My eyelids were hot as tar. I shut them tightly hoping that when I opened them, my real mom would be back. A choir of people's voices echoed in my head. *Your mom is so cool. Your mom is unlike any other mom in the whole town.* A part of me agreed with them. The rest of me crawled into myself and lay dormant for years.

The Rabbit

"Wanna come watch a movie?" Jeff's name, *burke45*, bubbles up next to the tiny green avatar that shows he's online. I'd only logged on seconds ago; not only did he message me first, but he's also invited me over.

Late winter's unrelenting arm has covered everything in frost. Outside is still. The frenetic energy of barn parties and late-night pool-hopping has been confined to Jeff's basement. Mrs. Burke, Jeff's mom, is the only mom (besides my own) in our group of friends that is "cool enough" to let us drink. She is much more relaxed compared with my mother's curiosity that keeps her hovering around us. Some of the girls who were friends of the guys before we came along have started calling Lex and me "groupies," a label that makes us write scathing LiveJournal entries in passive-aggressive response. But most weekends Lex and I indulge in the derogatory noun, blissful and ignorant.

We sip beers around the guys while they practice new songs. Lex dates Jeff for a few weeks, then splits up with him. I eyeball all of them like a glittering buffet. As if I'm starving from years of neglect, I wonder how many of them I can scoop onto my flimsy plate. The hulking desktop in front of me buzzes and hums with the weight of the internet while I wait in silence for a perfect response to surface.

@burke45 is typing…

"My mom's home, but she doesn't mind if we drink and hang," Jeff continues. He says his friends Lucas and Ashley will be there, and that I should meet them because "they're really cool. they don't drink or anything, they're totally straight edge." Friends at this movie night? So, it's not a date.

Jeff knows that I didn't drink a ton before I met the guys. His biggest tip-off, other than me ending most nights in tears over my crush on Sully, is the damn red flush that I'm still trying to bleach from my face each weekend. I haven't unloaded my life story to Jeff yet about my mom's unquenchable thirst for pinot grigio by the liter, but we have an unspoken understanding that we are cut from similar cloth.

The Burkes have an open-door policy. For the hundred or so times that I've been in Jeff's basement, Mrs. Burke has always stayed upstairs. She is the orbital parental figure who allows our illegal hangs, but she never tiptoes downstairs to try to be one of us. The handful of times we have come up for air have been unearthly experiences. Leaving the comfort of Jeff's basement to go to the cool, dark kitchen where Mrs. Burke sipped wine felt like a spacewalk in a parallel universe. Downstairs, only friends my age exist, jumping around to the Dropkick Murphys with 40s of malt liquor duct-taped to our hands. It's a realm where we'd "punch" each other in the crotch to prove some sort of gender equality, and it felt ridiculous when I'd walk upstairs and see there was an entire family up there watching primetime tv and doing their homework.

The first time I was in Mrs. Burke and Jeff's presence, I saw him shift uncomfortably from foot to foot. She mentioned an anecdote about little "Jeffrey" as a baby. With glowing love and adoration, she held our attention, delivered a punch line, and we all laughed. Mrs. Burke had the manners of Queen Elizabeth II in comparison to what I was used to, but I know that foot-shuffle well. It's the weight re-organization of the child of an alcoholic parent. The hip change is bracing for the inevitable downfall of their parent's goofy anecdote on glass three, which might topple down into a mess of tears and thrown china by glass five. I started to love Jeff then, in the eerie fluorescent light of Mrs. Burke's dated kitchen.

I realize I've been typing a response to Jeff and deleting it for a minute now, which he could see. The fear of being alone with Jeff is too much to bear, so I call Lex. Even though she has a history with him, it feels like enough time has passed. She is also my best friend. I need advice.

Lex arrives at my house already put together. After the first barn party, we rarely dally in the getting-ready processes that other teen girls live for. I like how efficient we have become. By getting all the t-zone blotting, lipstick lining, and outfit changing out of the way separately, we can get right into the belly of the night once together. Why waste a second polishing each other's nails when there is a basement filled with half-drunk boys to engage with? We are anxious to be in their company the second we part ways after the last school bell. The pull to be around them is so strong, I wonder why I haven't felt this kind of kinship with other friends.

Lex idles in my driveway, excited and smelling sweet. It's less than a two-minute drive up my street, across the road, and down Jeff's driveway to his front door, but the soundtrack has already been chosen. We want to swoop into view with the last thirty seconds of Thrice's "The Artist in the Ambulance" blasting on max. Most of the guys will be in the basement, music likely as high as ours. But in case someone is on the porch having a cigarette we need to prove that we are also casual listeners of post-hardcore.

Lex and I have never discussed this strategy aloud, but our fingers touch the dials at the same speed. Our timing has been perfected by years of watching shitty rom-coms. Everything about our outward appearance and tastes have been groomed to abide by the hormonal pull to the male sex. Sure, our punk-rock credo breaks some high school standards, but we hold fast to the same limiting gender norms as everyone else. Without explicitly saying it, these guys desired women who don't try hard — or at least would never admit to doing so — while they also longed for girlfriends who could check all the boxes of their action-film heroines. An impossible double standard.

Halfway between our houses, 0.2 miles away from each other, lies Highway 7, the main vein of Markham, which has two fast-moving lanes on each side. Once you get to each side of Highway 7, you're in suburban safety. But for a few seconds on that stretch of road, you're vulnerable to the speeding patrons of our town. It's not easy to drive straight through Highway 7; a heavy traffic day means you could wait minutes before crossing.

Lex and I bob our heads side to side, looking for oncoming traffic in solidarity to the Thrice song we know Jeff loves. We finally pull across the street during a lull, and that's when I see it.

"Lex — stop."

"What the fuck? I'm in the middle of the road."

"Stop! There're no cars. Is that a fucking bunny?"

"What the fuck?"

"It's a fucking hare or something! Stop!"

Lex pulls her car to the other side of Highway 7, and we get out. Our studded belts sag our corduroy boyfriend jeans. A fluffy, grey, twitching rabbit is lying in a pool of its own blood. It's still alive.

"We need to save it," says Lex.

"Do you think we should touch it?"

"Is rabies still a thing?"

We realize we have nothing that we can use to scoop up the rabbit, so we scoot our tiny bodies back into her car and finish the drive to

Jeff's front door. We knock with the purpose of a police squad. We hope the Highway 7 traffic is kind in the next few minutes. The last thirty seconds of "Artist in the Ambulance" rings out in the night like we planned, but no one is on the porch. Jeff's straight-edge friends finally open the door to our pounding.

"Hi, uh, like, we need like, a fucking towel — STAT."

My voice is stronger and louder than I normally have the cadence for. Their boozeless lifestyle, sleeve tattoos, face piercings, and 00 ear gauges are enough to terrify anyone, but tonight a dying rabbit trumps all priors.

Jeff goofily comes bouncing into view, and I try to ignore that his confused smile widens when he sees Lex.

"Jeff," she says, "Can we borrow a towel? We found a dead rabbit."

"Actually you might not get it ba—" I cut myself off because Jeff has already hurried out of view. He comes back with a pink and yellow beach towel.

"Uhhh, okay, you girls are fucking nuts." Jeff's only looking at Lex, and it dawns on me that he misses her.

Lex and I swing back, and luckily the rabbit hasn't been pulverized by minivans yet. On the contrary, the rabbit's body is like a shedding of itself. A hollowed-out shell barely clinging to muscle memory. We grab it with the lush beach towel and pop it in the back seat.

"What the fuck do we do now?"

Back at Jeff's, the guys are emerging from the basement to go to the porch, but our mix CD has switched to Dashboard Confessional. We turn down the volume when we approach.

We can hear them before we see them, the jingle of keys attached via carabiner to low-slung jeans.

An almost silent swish of long hair swings into view. It's Dave, Copeland, and Marley.

"Yo, we're about to have a smoke. What's good?" asks Marley.

"I'll go get it," Lex says.

I fumble in my purse to find my mom's gift of DuMaurier Reds, and I follow them on the porch. I tuck a cigarette behind my large ear, and it falls out immediately. I try to catch it with my hand, but I end up launching it further down the driveway. Hurriedly, I scoop the cigarette up and shove it into my mouth, lighting it backwards. Choking on the melted filter, a bit of rabbit's blood is not only on my hands but now in my mouth. A row of eyes stare at Lex and me. They're waiting for a performance of some kind.

I hear Mrs. Burke inside in the kitchen. Jeff isn't anywhere. I try my best to summarize the last fifteen minutes in a cool and calm manner, but halfway through explaining "finding roadkill" and "trying to resuscitate roadkill" I realize how stupid of a task this is. Lex knows this before I do, and when Jeff finally appears on the porch, they chat on the side about watching a movie.

"Well," Copeland says, chucking a finished dart into the lawn. "We need to save the little guy. Let's go."

"Wait — go where?"

"I dunno? Main Street Village Vet is close to us."

It hadn't occurred to me that we'd actually try and bring this half-dead rabbit to an institution to save it. I imagined it hopping back into the forest, after a little belly rub and maybe a carrot. Of course, the trauma is palpable. The rabbit would not survive without the help of a professional.

There's a shift I can feel. I know it well from being a single girl entwined with the lackadaisical comfort couples have. The indifferent homebodies versus the fired-up spirit of the usually more drunk, single kids.

"Yeah, actually, I don't want to do that," says Lex. She's always so straightforward with her needs and desires. I envy this, along with everything else about her.

"Yeah, that's dumb. Let's go watch the movie," follows Jeff.

At this moment, I get sole custody of the dying rabbit. I know I would look foolish to follow them inside, even though that's all I want to do. So, I commit. Lex disappears into the house with Jeff, Lucas, and Ashley. I'm left outside with the other guys and the shivering roadkill. Copeland offers me a swig of his rye while he, Dave, and Marley carry the rabbit to their van.

I close my eyes on Jeff's porch and think about the comfort of his arm around me. Could I see it, though? The flirting, the movie watching, the chitter-chatter of straight-edge life. I feel better knowing that I'd be outed so fast, knowing zero point zero about punk music. Like so many times before in my life, I shame and console myself with a hundred reasons why I am a terrible candidate for love.

"Okay, let's do this!" Copeland yells.

I turn my back on Jeff's house and get into Dave's van. It's cold and uncomfortable. It's not just the dying animal, I also know the vet clinic is closed and that this night will have a dismal ending for the rabbit and me. Dave starts his car, and a song comes on that's unfamiliar. Dave has already gone to college, so we haven't spent much time together outside of band practice. He buckles in his seatbelt and motions for me to do the same.

"Ready to save this probably already-dead rabbit?"

"FUCKING YES!" Copeland shouts from the back seat. Chuckles from Marley. Dave looks at me, waiting.

"Let's do it," I say.

I try to study Dave's profile as we drive in the night, his little soul-patch catching the amber street lights every few seconds. He has a girlfriend, Evelyn, who everyone teases him about because she's a few years younger. That fact has usually stopped me from registering anything more in my fluctuating hormonal brain about him, but in my attempt to erase Jeff, a blank spot is emerging. My hooded sweatshirt allows my eyes to explore his high cheekbone ledges and his handsome face secretly. His hairline is strong and sure of itself. His soft brown hair is the type that I can tell will thin one day, but now it's undulating and silky. I already have too much heartache with Sully and Jeff as leading stars in my journals. I wonder if I can take one more unrequited love right now.

When we pull up to the empty parking lot of Main Street Village Vet, I notice lace-scalloped curtains closing off the windows of the Tudor-style office building. Snow drifts in little haphazard spirals, and I suddenly feel like the big bad wolf at a storybook grandmother's house. Or, were we the heroes? Would we be welcomed with astonished applause? Would we receive a cash reward? A write-up in the local paper at least? Fluorescent lights flicker from the strip mall beside us, washing my idyllic scene with a radioactive hue.

Now the only girl in the gang, I am compelled to live up to the gusto I charged in with at the start of the night. I cradle the dying rabbit as I walk up the front steps. The pastel beach towel wrapped around the rabbit is the kind that Costco pumps out, so plush and large that you can barely feel your own body when rubbing it down, let alone that of a frail and unmoving bunny. I peek into the pocket we made, checking to make sure the rabbit is still in the folds. I look down at the small face of a bloodied Peter Rabbit, whiskers slicked down, tiny mouth exhaling its last breaths. I have an urge to squeeze it out of its misery and end the crusade here.

It's hard to miss the front door's orange block letters spelling out that they're *CLOSED — Call Again Soon*. I knock meekly. Nothing. I knock again, a little less meekly. I worry about startling the rabbit.

"Someone's in there!" whisper-yells Copeland, who's standing about fifty yards behind me, lighting up a cigarette. I knock a third time, and a silhouette comes to the door. The person could have been a doctor, a nurse, or a janitor, but we are relieved someone might help us after all.

A woman peers through the curtain, taking stock of the scene. Her eyes bolt between my raccoon- ringed eyeliner and Copeland's scowl, lit by cigarette. Her eyebrows crumple in confusion. I hold up the rabbit then, to which she raises her eyebrows in alarm. She swings the lace curtains closed. The lights turn off.

"What. The FUCK!?" Copeland has shed his whisper. "Piece-of-shit vet clinic willing to let this animal die? Mother FUCKERS. We gotta call the police."

I do the math quickly. We are soaked enough in alcohol that it doesn't matter if Dave is the sober driver. We aren't of age yet, and we are technically trespassing at this hour.

"Um, that's okay, Copeland. Let's just go back," I say as I feel the animal quiver in my hands. "I do think it might finally be over for this little buddy."

We halfheartedly toss around a few more options and vet clinics, and then someone mentions that we might still be able to make it back in time for the movie at Jeff's. I know I still have time to get into that basement before the movie is over, anyway.

Dave tells us to wait by the curb. He's going to do this on the Main Street Village Vet property to make a statement. Copeland, Marley, and I stand aside while Dave positions the almost-carcass a few yards ahead of his front tire, enough room to get some momentum. We mutter a couple suggestions from a distance: "a little further," and "a little to the left." My feeble attempt to participate makes me feel less guilty that I'm actually more focused on how much time might be left of the movie.

The headlights turn on, and Dave buckles up and hits the gas.

For such a tiny thing, the crunch of the tires is louder than I'd expected. It reverberates in all of our bones. I turn into Copeland as he angrily inhales a drag. "Fuckers," he repeats. I gesture for his cigarette, and I make it disappear with one long inhale.

No one inside the clinic notices our protest, and I'm ready to be back in the safety of Jeff's basement, even if it does come bundled with all my insecurities. I can't tell if I'm sobering up too fast, but the real world feels so razor sharp, I feel like the curb is cutting my ankles. I've seen dead raccoons, foxes, and rabbits in my backyard my whole life, but somehow this death feels unfair.

To any passerby, we might have looked like the poster children for bad influences, with our metal accessories, cigarettes, and drunk fists held to the sky. But all we wanted was for this helpless being to have a shot at survival. We weren't naive. We knew there were 100 cars hitting 100 rabbits at that very moment, but *we* picked up *this one*.

We climb back into Dave's van, silent and pissed off. I tell myself not to look at the pile of entrails on the way in, but I do.

"Where's Copeland?" one of us asks.

And then I see it: a cartoon-like, perfectly sized, rust-colored brick sailing through the air. My mouth hangs open and mouths "no," but it's too late. The deafening crash of brick hitting glass leads to a million little shards raining down like chimes on the black pavement. I hope to any god that no one is behind the window.

Copeland jumps into the van yelling, "Go! Go! Go!" When I see his face, I immediately forgive him. Dave peels out of the parking lot and drives past Jeff's house, past the train tracks, and past the light of town. We finally let out a laugh when we realize there's no police car chasing us, but it felt good to drive so fast in the night. We pretend we're on the run anyway. Dave turns up the music until the speakers shake, and I keep the sound of rabbit bones crunching inside of me, where I can keep it safe.

We return to Jeff's to find Lex curled up with him on the couch in a clear signal of back-togetherness. I slump my body onto the chair furthest from them, hoping to hide my disappointment behind the rabbit's doom.

"How'd it go?" one of them asks.

"Dave ran it over, Copeland threw a brick through the window," one of us returns.

"That's fucked up."

Jeff turns the volume back up, and we divert our attention back to the movie.

That night, I dream that when my teeth gnash together, my mouth is crushing the rabbit's body. My molars fall out. My hands cover my mouth to catch them. Opening my palms, I see no teeth. Only tiny rabbit bones turning to dust.

Cornell Park Avenue

I won't find out until years later how rare it is for a father to get sole custody of his children. Kyle, Dakota and I never saw a courtroom or met our parents' lawyers. We only got hints of the truth from their short phrases like, "Mom's moving out," and "We still love you exactly the same."

Divorce discussions came up periodically at the breakfast table or during school drop-offs. Mostly harmless passive-aggressive comments were tossed around about the other parent's post-divorce life. Mom's curiosity was stronger than my dad's. Her relentless questions about "Christman Court" — what we called our childhood home after the divorce — led my siblings and me to believe that she might have still loved our father even after they called it quits.

Even though Mom was already onto boyfriend number two by the time I was in high school, my siblings and I, like so many kids of separated parents, picked apart her every word for a hint of leftover love.

"So, how much did *your father* give you for your birthday this year?"

"How much money do you think *your father* is bringing home these days?"

"What friends did *your father* see over the weekend?"

"Does *your father* talk about me with his sisters and brothers anymore?"

Mom's questions usually involved money or my parents' former social circles. I really didn't understand her obsession with money. From what I knew, she "got half" of whatever my dad had, plus a new house of her choice. If what our parents told us was true, that divorces led to a "better life" and "happier times ahead," buying a brand-new house seemed like the cherry on top.

Shopping for a new home for a parent was not something I ever envisioned, except maybe decades down the line when they were both elderly and in need of a smaller living space. I imagined my dad at home in his chair while a grey-haired Mom toured condos in Florida with me on our annual future girls' trips. The heat and sun flare would hide her wrinkled face and any trace of sadness. But in her early forties, Mom was still a beautiful woman — and still sharp around the edges.

She was as in-focus as a person could be. She still got a haircut and color every eight weeks. Her hair was shorter and spikier than ever, shifting from auburn to a deep plum red. With her rippling green eyes, she resembled Jessica Rabbit with a pixie cut. If she was mad, excited, happy, or depressed, I could see it on her line-free face from a mile away. Even though her reputation was tarnished from her many run-ins with local police, she was still the most interesting person in any room. At busy open houses, realtors would flirt with her and ignore everyone else. At interior design studios, she'd come close to getting hired before they found out she didn't make it past ninth grade. Mom exuded a savvy, business-like manner, and then within seconds she'd have the room bent in half, laughing at her crude jokes. She was an electric current that drew us all in —and delighted in shocking us when we got too close.

Mom decided to move to Cornell, a new development in Markham that was bounded by a country sideroad and Highway 7. Mom and Dad's divorce became official when I turned thirteen, and my parents tried to sweeten the deal with all the usual treats: Two Christmases! Two Thanksgivings! Two summer vacations! But our most extravagant justification gift was Mom's choice of a second home. It was a brand-new build only a few minutes' drive from Christman Court. Even though we were only at Mom's house Wednesday afternoons and every other weekend, our time with her ticked too slowly and returned too fast. The few minutes between houses might as well have been a hundred miles. Just before she moved out, she had permanently lost her driver's license, thanks to the impaired driving "three-strikes and you're out" law. Relying on taxis and her boyfriend's pickup trucks to shuttle us around, she filled the moat around her to the brim. Unless it was time for our dad to come claim us, getting out of Cornell was never easy.

Soon after Mom bought the place in Cornell, we started the duplication process. I didn't realize how much stuff I had until I started to furnish my room at Mom's place. Since she hated to shuttle our things between houses, she demanded that we buy an alternate wardrobe, a second winter coat, and toiletries. If she saw any extra luggage carried from Christman Court, she inspected what was inside, taxied us to the mall, and bought a version of it for the Cornell house. After just a few weeks, the pleasures that came with buying something new started to fade.

Cornell had been rural farmland before it exploded into a planned community of thousands of suburbanites. Most Cornell builds were three or more stories tall, with separate garages at the rear, connected by a tiny, ten-by-ten pad of lawn. Within a year, we saw Cornell mutate from cornfields to mountains of excavated fill, to rows of cookie-cutter, Victorian-style homes. My mom chose a four-story townhome with ten-foot ceilings on the main boulevard.

For all her pining over the loss of Christman Court, my siblings and I wondered why she chose a place so radically different from our old home. Christman Court was a modest ranch with an acre of lawn and wild English gardens. Cornell Park Avenue was an imitation Brooklyn sprinkled with Stepford Wives charm. If I had been listening, I might have heard Mom say she was done with taking care of a home that required so much maintenance. I might have heard her say her hands and back were tired from gardening all weekend. I might have heard her say she didn't need big tubs to bathe us grown kids in anymore. I imagined she was looking forward to a future where she could play a liberated housewife, a fantasy she repeated to us often. If I had been listening, I might have heard her say that since she couldn't duplicate the door frames of our childhood bedrooms, the ones she'd carefully etched our heights into, she wanted her new home to look nothing like Christman Court.

Mom beamed with a feverous excitement for the few weeks we attended open houses with her.

"I get to start from scratch! Design my own home! Did you see that open-concept kitchen? Screw it, I'm getting the $500 bar stools. You kids pick out anything you want. *Anything*. Kyle, you want bunk beds? This isn't Dad's house, this is *mine*."

Her enthusiasm was infectious. We'd race to finish homework so we could scan *Architectural Digest* and help her design her new kitchen. I picked out a four-poster bed, the kind I'd always dreamt of, with gauzy curtains that I could close around me. We spent most weekends in furniture showrooms, tile shops and IKEAs. Kyle, Dakota and I loved every second of our design quest. We felt like little adults schlepping giant, cobalt-blue bags filled with hooks, mirrors, and throw blankets. Each swipe of Mom's credit card prompted a comforting pat on our heads that warmed us when we tucked ourselves inside the chilly new bed covers. As was the style then, we dressed the big bay windows in sheer chiffon curtains that accentuated the breezy, open-concept style she loved. Unfortunately, my bedroom faced Cornell Park Avenue's new LED streetlights, bathing my walls in bright white all through the night. It didn't matter how deeply I burrowed into my goose down duvet; there wasn't anywhere to hide while sleeping under a spotlight.

Mom moved to Cornell on a January morning, when she hit an all-time high with her giddiness. Having chugged enough coffee to power the town, she buzzed from room to room, making each one as comfortable as possible for us. She even laid out "jammies" on our beds, the way she used to when we were little. Even though her teeth gleamed in a permanent smile, I caught a trembling anytime Dakota scanned her room a little too long. Being only seven, Dakota was our truth-teller by way of her childlike, inhibition-less mind.

"Ooh! It's really clean and bare in here," Dakota said before adding, "I mean modern! Okay, maybe if I put my stuffed animals like this, it will add more colors." While Dakota rearranged her toys on her bedspread, I saw windshield wipers swipe across Mom's unblinking eyes.

"Of course it's not going to be as *cozy* as Dad's house yet, but that's because we need to live in it more! Throw clothes on the chair. Roast some chicken dinners, right?"

The sun set so early in January that it was barely four o'clock when Mom began her happy hour ritual. Her boyfriend, Mac, had dutifully stocked the fridge with white wine and beers. To this day, when I think of him, I can smell the liquor store we frequented as a new family. The one in our town was a redemption center, beer shop combination. I can smell the reek of old cans being returned and hear the clinking of bottles jangle in my head when I picture his ruddy face. He was quick to smile and generally pleasant, but too eager to please and his expressions quickly turned sour and distrustful when we tested him, which was often.

When we found out they were together, Kyle and I used our rudimentary Microsoft Paint skills to draw his face on a Big Mac sandwich. We hoped that our cruelty would drive him away, but Mac would outlast all three of us. We couldn't fathom this then, still in the vacuum of our youth, when Mom was the center of our universe. Plus, we were too busy inflating hope for her with short, affirmative sentences.

"This place is so cool! You're going to love making friends here! We'll visit your house all the time," we reassured her.

"This isn't just my place, it's *our* place. It's your home too."

There were a few roads that led to my mom's unraveling. Sometimes, it was the slow, hand-wringing hours between her first and second bottle of wine. We never saved corks in our houses; bottle stoppers as cocktail-host gifts were eyeroll-worthy. Along this particular road, Kyle, Dakota and I watched, darting our eyes from the TV to her wine glass, as she paced back and forth to the kitchen for smoke breaks. She only smoked once or twice during the first bottle, but she'd start to chain smoke by the second. There was a correlation between her drunkenness and the temperature of the tips of our noses. During winter, how cold we felt was directly related to how many times she opened the window to have another cigarette. We measured each step of Mom's slow inebriation by the number of inappropriate jokes she told. By glass four, her words started to sag and lose their shape. The happy tears came around glass six, the despondent crying soon after.

All the while, we stayed rooted beside our mom, clinging to her every moment. We were doting babysitters hoping that our presence might remind her to slow down. Of course, we rarely told her out loud to stop drinking, for fear of her usual recourse: faster drinking. So, we stayed positive, shared stories, and making inappropriate jokes in response to hers. We hung onto the mechanical bull for as long as we could. When we felt proud of how many minutes we'd mastered, the operator would smile and crank the speed up, tossing us off the bull the moment we reached for the tips of our noses.

Another road to Mom's unraveling were the times we couldn't count her sips of wine because we were out with friends or playing in the park. This road was darker, meaner. This road gave us whiplash like a scene-switch in a horror movie. Kids went soaring high on swing sets, or ran in fields to an eerily upbeat soundtrack, but the viewer knew something was lurking in the background while they played.

In those precious hours of backyard time, or dinners in the living rooms of other kids' families, we were worry-free. Free from conversations about bitches and drunks. Free from hearing about the various abuses Mom had suffered as a child. When I was at my friends' houses, I never tucked their parents into bed. I never had to line trash cans with extra plastic bags and tell them it was all going to be okay in the morning. I never had to sneak phone calls to my dad and whisper that he needed to come and get us again.

My sister, brother, and I got back to Cornell Park Avenue late and hungry. No matter how wasted mom was, she almost always had impeccable meals ready for us. We braced ourselves imagining that this time she might only be a little tipsy. This hope was as relentless as it was useless.

From the moment we walked inside one such evening, we knew something was off because there were no smells of buttered onions or poached salmon. No lights were on, and *Home & Garden TV* wasn't playing in the background. Mac wasn't there. My stomach flipped for a second thinking of the worst-case scenario — the scenario she had hinted might happen so many times in my life. The scenario that I walked into once when I was eight. The scenario that led me to try to pronounce the words on a pill bottle to the warbled voice of a 911 operator.

But that scene evaporated when we heard Mom shuffling in the kitchen. There was a telltale clink of a wine stem hitting the countertop, followed by a forceful pour of pinot. We could tell by the sound of the liquid rushing into the glass and the velocity at which the splashes escaped the rim that this was likely the end of the second or third bottle. She was still in her winter coat, her makeup smudged under her eye.

"Oh, you're finally here, *Mom's housssuh.*" She gestured to the kitchen around her. The extra syllable at the end of 'house' settled into our silence.

My siblings and I didn't physically touch, but our minds connected with the same message: *stay together*. As much as one of us might have given anything to hide in our rooms, running away meant more of Mom concentrated on the remaining siblings. After all, no matter how much she drank, Mom could still turn the doorknob to our bedroom. What we would have given for a trap door hidden somewhere that only we kids knew, and that she couldn't find. How long would she search for us before she gave up? The sheer endurance of her spilling her guts to us while we tried to sleep was formidable. She could be blacked out, but she'd still spend hours on the end of each of our beds telling discursive tales of ex-lovers, how bad our dad was, and how ungrateful we were.

"What's for dinner?" I smiled, trying to keep it light. *Shit.* "Oh, I mean, can I help with dinner?"

"What's for dinner? Fuck you, that's what's for dinner."

"It's okay, Mom!" Dakota swooped in. She was barely a toddler a few years ago, but at this point she had the emotional intelligence of an adult. "Let's cook it together now! It'll be fun!"

Mom gazed at Dakota the same way I'd seen her stare at her since her daughter's birth. She recognized something in Dakota that she didn't see in me. Her blurry stare was more than registering Dakota's blonde compared to my black hair; it was something deep-rooted that was only theirs.

"My golden girl," Mom gushed, a few tears spilling over her eyelids. "You are so helpful to your mommy."

We wouldn't make dinner together that night, but at least there wouldn't be wine glasses shattered on the walls. No police would be called. No neighbors would crowd the lawn with raised eyebrows. That night we watched our mom crouch on the carpet of the living room while she wailed. We shut our eyes and mouths, and we took turns patting her back. The new gas fireplace was the only light in the den, and it illuminated the grief in her face like a ghoul. I stared only at the flames, too embarrassed to look at her.

The fire barely kept us warm in the cathedral-like house that still smelled like fresh paint. She threw her arms up and down like a servant bowing, begging for her life. She dragged her fingers along the carpet, screaming. Each time she flung herself up and back down again, her winter coat inched closer and closer to the hot glass of the fireplace. I stood up to turn it off, but I stopped halfway and got back on my knees beside her. I might have been too exhausted, too depleted to tell her she might burn herself.

I counted the minutes until they became hours. In our telepathic imaginations, my siblings and I asked each other if we should call our dad to pick us up. Mom would eventually get tired from crying. But even if we could escape, how could we leave her like this? Accepting our lose-lose situation, we stayed silent and still, stone-children waiting for their turn to be tucked in. Our eyes locked on the fire, possessed by a hope that she might burn herself without us having to push her into the flames.

Shitty Bar

"I don't think we should compare moms," Jeff says. I'm sitting with him on a dewy field near our rival high school. Since our houses are so close, we often walk home together when we're not drinking in his basement. Our other usual hangout is Shitty Bar, a semi-wide permanent trailer that serves under-aged kids bottles of Heineken for $2. It technically has some other name, like Corner Pocket Grill & Bar or some other take on billiards, but the owners never light up the broken neon sign. The bartenders sometimes put porn on TVs that are bolted into the corners. It looks more like a construction manager's sad, onsite office than a bar.

Any assortment of Jeff, Sully, Lex, Dave, Marley, Copeland, and I shoot pool there, trying not to stare at the orgies in the background. These are among our first times ever being served at a bar, playing snooker, sliding the back door open for smoke breaks. At Shitty Bar, we get the chance to role-play the grown-up life of freedom that we had dreamt of since childhood. While chesty blondes moan in the background, we saunter around with our pool cues, acting like the adults we want to be. We count our cash and buy each other $10 rounds, laughing about who threw up the hardest the night before, and who might cry the hardest tonight. That's when they all raise their eyebrows, chuckle, and with some love point to me. Once we finish our R-rated play, and the TVs' explicit content gets too weird, we wander into the night hoping the buzz will last as long as we do.

"I know we have some similar stories," I continue, feeling the grass between my fingers. "But your mom is so put together, so loving and nice. Lex tells me all the time how much she loves your mom." Jeff thinks for a moment, his eyebrows knit at the highest point of his forehead. I shouldn't have brought up Lex or his mom, but they're who I think about when we're alone together.

"Yeah, but that doesn't take away from the fact that I can't trust her to stay sober for very long. She's always sad, and my dad sucks. At least you have a cool dad."

"I'm done with cool parents. I want boring parents. I want curfews and dinners at the kitchen table where we talk about stupid shit, like what we want to be when we grow up."

We laugh, recalling when Marley was asked by Lex's strict and very intimidating father what he wanted to study in college. Marley "replied" by inhaling a cigarette, exhaling the cigarette, grunting, and finally saying — "the fuck knows."

Jeff has been steadily dating Lex for most of the school year. Since I'm her best friend, and close-enough to Jeff, I've experienced most of their relationship secondhand. Each milestone, momentous or mundane, I've listened to with a gritted smile so tight that my jaw constantly feels sore.

One night, when we couldn't get into Shitty's, we lit a fire deep in the woods that connected to my backyard. Lex told me that she and Jeff had finally slept together. Her face morphed in the flame light, from bewildered to excited, and back again. As she went through all the details of their night, my stomach bubbled hot with heartburn and reflux splashed at my throat. In the safety of the darkness, my eyes darted across the forest floor where Jeff sat with Sully and his new girlfriend.

An intense sadness swept through me then, and it took all my energy to push it back down. Liquor helped suppress the feeling at first, but it always brought the pain right back up with my dinner. By the end of the night, I was usually slumped over a bottle of Jack Daniels, crying on the curb. For all the confidence that I built up in finding and creating this species of teen, I still slowly succumbed to my self-pity. I was the same hand-wringing, depressed girl I'd been before I met these guys.

As we approached the end of the year, photography became a little pinprick of light in the dark rooms of my identity. I zombied around taking pictures at home, or during the late-night bonfires. I didn't consider that "photographer" could be a viable career option until my senior year. My Comms & Tech teacher said that he liked the photos I took of Jeff and Sully's band. He suggested I take more portraits of my friends and family members as practice. Having more images "in my portfolio" was a great thing for college, he added.

Though I claimed that my photography was for school, I began to use the camera as my excuse to spend time alone with Jeff and Sully before I went away to college. In a not-so-subtle move, I photographed Sully atop a tombstone at my favorite cemetery to signify that he was "dead to me." I offered the obligatory couples photo shoot to Jeff and Lex, with the caveat that I also needed their solo portraits.

On my favorite day of this self-administered project, I photographed Jeff in the middle of Highway 7. He sat straddling the double yellow markings of the pavement, surrounded by clementine rinds. When shit got too real at home, I'd log onto messenger and find him. After unloading about my latest family dramas, I see him type one word as a question: *clementines?* And then he'd show up in the middle of the highway with a bag of tiny oranges for me, which we peeled and ate together. This small orange fruit was something that only we shared, and I was careful to justify it with a paper-thin argument about "progressive" views on platonic male-female relationships.

By the end of summer, I was developing film on my own at a shop in town. As my friends' faces emerged from the developer chemicals, I felt a surge of confidence resurface in me. For so much of my youth,

I assumed "outcast" was a label I'd be doomed to wear forever. Then I found this group of misfits. But they weren't really misfits, or outcasts, or even punks. In fact, I had been so obsessed with labeling our place in the world, I nearly missed the most important part of being a kid: the freedom that comes with not caring about labels at all.

"What time is it?" I ask. Both of our phones are dead.

"By the estimate of the star placement, something like 1 or 4 am," Jeff replies with his signature sarcastic smile.

"Ha. Ha."

We lean back and take in the starry sky. So many of our adventures have taken place at night, yet we've rarely bothered to look up. Something about being horizontal with Jeff now feels intrusive, bordering on illicit. It's August, but it's cold tonight. The dampness of the new morning soaks our black hoodies. The second a shiver leaves my body, I regret it. Jeff puts his arm around me, and I close my eyes. Once I'm in the crook of his arm, my body adjusts to the heat coming off of him. I shiver harder, and he pulls me closer. I try to think of something to say before we do anything I'll regret.

"Do you think you're going to marry Lex?" *Fuck. Why did I say that?*

"I don't know," he replies quietly. "I don't know."

We're quiet, staring upward and thinking about the question and the answer, when a shooting star fizzles through the black.

"Oh my god!" we both say.

"Did you see that?" we both say.

Quiet. Our eyes leap around the celestial scene, looking for clues to where it might have come from, and where it might have gone.
"That was the first time I've seen a shooting star," Jeff tells me after

a moment. This surprises me, because his half-sleeve tattoo is a lyric from a song about a shooting star.

"No fucking way. How is that possible? You're eighteen, and this is your first shooting star?"

"Yeah, not kidding."

"Well, let's hope for another one," I say, and I settle back into his side body. The star has granted me some signal, the dust-ejaculate of some twisted fairy godmother telling me that I *belonged* beside him. This moment is the pinnacle of an entire year of my imagined diary entries. In all my years of being the weeper, the girl who wrote unanswered letters to actors, the last pick on the team, the moon-face mascot, the girl with the home that "smelled Chinese," the girl with the unruly hair, and the mother so disappointed in all of the above, finally there is a boy beside me who wants my company.

I'm ready to do the worst thing imaginable, but on that knoll, no repercussions enter my mind because my life's shortcomings are chips I trade in for this moment. I ignore the pain I'll inflict on Lex because for what I'm about to do, I am owed.

Jeff and I lie in silence for a few more minutes, waiting for another shooting star. The dew soaks into our clothes, and we both shiver until we are hugging again. His hand rubs my back, and I look up into his eyes, locking us in the body language that asks if the next move should happen or not. He doesn't budge, so I kiss him on his bottom lip. I expect him to roll away, disgusted with me and maybe with himself, but his eyes are closed. When he opens them, he looks deep in thought and disappointed. If there are more shooting stars that night, we miss them.

On the walk home, Jeff bombards me with questions. "What's wrong?" is the most annoying and repetitive one. *What do you fucking think is wrong?* I hope my silence will give him the space he needs to profess his love for me, or at least promise he'll break up with Lex, or even just guess that I love him. Instead, my silence just begets more silence.

Instead of parting ways at his house, we walk to a 24-hour coffee shop and share a small regular with what little change we have on us. We sit in the cemetery talking about nonsense, including my ridiculous obsession with Sully, in an attempt to erase what just happened. Then we meander toward our houses, not before stopping in the middle of Highway 7. We lie down, finding a crook between the thickly painted yellow strokes to lay our spines along. The raised parallel lines hold us upright, sneaker soles touching and arms behind the napes of our skulls. A few whooshing cars honk as they speed past us.

Jeff will tell her first. We agree on this before we part ways that night. We are both her best friends, after all.

***

After Jeff reveals what happened between us, Lex and I don't speak for almost a month. She and Jeff continue, steady and strong, from what I can see at least. Their inner workings are now shielded from me entirely. If they did fight, which I imagine they must have, they don't tell me. I am cut from the trio we once had. They date for years after that summer, and though the three of us become friendly again, our closeness evaporates, and we use our distances as excuses for our separation.

Lex and I eventually heal our friendship altogether. I recite a few pitiful monologues and send her letters that decry my brokenness. I tell her I don't know how to love people, but she knows this already, which is why I think she forgives me. If the situation was reversed, I know I wouldn't have.

My journal entries about Jeff and Sully end after that summer too. Starting college at a school 450 miles away help me pull the barbs of their studded belts from my skin. I meet new boys and chase after them. A few return my love, but the unrequited years of my youth linger as a deep scar for a long time. I eventually get a face piercing of my own: an eyebrow stud. It falls out one night, and I re-pierce it before it heals properly. I laugh at myself in the mirror, watching a metaphor incarnate.

The guys of my high school youth are finally behind me, but there is a deeper wound that I've inflicted on myself after tearing my body into two parts. This wound still pulsates from the battleground in my core where my whiteness took a hammer to the Asian girl, who kept reappearing when it looked to be safe. It never was. The minorities of my generation were raised in a rigged, whack-a-mole game. With a wide smile, I empty my pockets under the bright carnival lights. I eagerly grab the mallet each time the mole presents itself, with the promise of another chance to fit in. Swinging with all my might at the grinning mammal, I never receive the satisfaction of ever hitting it.

I rarely visit my hometown anymore. The guys have all grown up and started families of their own. I re-read my old journals from 2004 and think about how much time I spent longing for a specific kind of love, crying on the curb, covered in stolen sherry, wet mascara chunks on my cheeks, Lex or one of the guys always there to dust me off and set me straight. If I didn't know the band playing, they'd make me CDs. If I didn't want to dance, I'd be pushed into the center of the crowd anyway. If I stared at my hair in disgust, hair products were suggested, Elmer's glue tossed in my lap. If I needed saving from my mom, Jeff's basement lights were always on. If I wanted to save a dying animal but couldn't, Dave took the wheel. There was love gushing out of every night of those months we lived under stars, in the dark.

When I do get the guts to drive though my old neighborhood, there's only one album I play. I can't tell if Madonna's *Ray of Light* got better with age, or if it was just the first punk album I ever heard. Hardcore audiophiles might disagree, since the main demographic for Madonna's "new-age techno" phase were middle-aged women of the suburbs. And it's true, when I hear it I can see Mom dancing in the ornate hydrangea-lined cage she built herself, in charge of three kids with a husband who was always gone, she escaped the only way she knew how. While we raged in mosh pits in abandoned barns and dank venues, Mom's speakers shook just as loud. At the right swell, Madonna's orchestra could carry Mom's own voice, which screamed to be let free. In the safety of its clamor, she thrashed her dance. All music that sets us free is punk music.

Now, when I drive along Highway 7, I roll my windows down, waiting for the scent of stale beer and clementines to greet me. Queuing up *Ray of Light*, I turn the volume up as loud as I can and put my hand out into the familiar air. I zoom around to the old houses where we lived that fractured last year of my youth. I drive the roads home from Shitty Bar. I slow down to see if the same vet clinic is there. I park beside the mound of lawn where a shooting star changed everything. I never drive by Emer's house. I always drive by Lex's house, sending a useless apology in the direction of the strangers who live there now. I play "Nothing Really Matters" at full blast until Madonna shakes my car, and in another world I'm dancing with my mom in the living room. I'm forgetting about my homework, forgetting what we look like to neighbors. I let her universe of crude heroines lead the way without judgment. We spin until we laugh, we laugh until we cry.

Although it wasn't the musical I was expecting, the guys brought a raucous sound into my life. Through a mosh-pit education, my gait became galvanized. In crowded rooms, I keep my elbows out, making space for myself. Whether I danced in my head, or in fowl disguise, every year, I landed a little louder, shaking the rooms as I entered them. I don't hang-wring anymore, I raise my hands and flaunt them to the sky.

And now I am now learning to love the red-flush of my collarbone when a battle ignites inside me. It's a signal that someone with something important to say is there, just underground.

I never would have seen them before. How have I never seen them before? They were here all along.

Acknowledgments

I owe immeasurable thanks to my sister and my brother. You stayed patient while I tried to mother you in-between writing love letters to David Duchovny. I'm so lucky to be bonded with you forever. Though we had to wade through trenches to get here, look at the shining swords we wield now.

For my father, who always nurtured the artists in us. Who saw me, flailing in those murky teenage waters, and taught me how to sail. From you, I learned that if I allowed it my life could be filled with adventure, friends, and love. Thank you for believing in me.

Speaking of love, Ian, I simply could not have done this without yours. Thank you for taking care of our family while I spent hours inside my head or away writing. You steered me steady. If I ever threw the pages to the ground, you always put them back in my lap, asking to hear more.

Thank you to my teachers, editors, muses, and research buddies. Thank you, Mr. Moskal, for showing me that a profession in film, media, and tech was possible, at just the right time in my life. Thank you to Heidi, for your incredibly diligent eye on these words.

To my cheering section: Uncle Christian, Uncle Dave, Louise, Rob, and Catherine. For Alex and Cara. You are my chosen sisters for life. I'm so lucky to have known you then, and now. To Morgan, for bringing sound and color into my Maine creative life. To Carole, who recognizes the reluctant daughter in me, yet tenderly stands nearby, with plane tickets and big ideas always at the ready.

For Dave, the only one who could put our rabbit to sleep that night. Your letters reignited this story just two years ago, but your belief in me since we were teens has always been formidable. Let's never stop being weird artists.

I am so grateful for the Maine Writers & Publishers Alliance, who saw a nervous new kid looking for a place to sit at the cafeteria and waved me over. The MWPA showed me that the path to where I wanted to go wasn't some magical land far away, but just a snow-covered road that needed some shoveling.

This is for every kid or adult-child who has lost a parent to an alcohol-related illness. I am in awe of you who hung on and healed, I am humbled by you who had to let go in distance or in death. Unfortunately, you're not alone; fortunately, you're not ever alone.

Of course, there is only really one person I'm talking to when I write about these years of my life. I promise to never write in spite of you, Mom, only in search of. Love you always.

About the
Maine Writers & Publishers Alliance

Founded in 1975 by a group of small presses and writers, Maine Writers & Publishers Alliance (MWPA) has worked for decades to enrich the literary life and culture of Maine. We bring together Maine writers, editors, publishers, booksellers, and literary professionals at all stages of their careers to sharpen craft, create community, and celebrate great writing. MWPA has an active, growing membership of more than 1,500 literary professionals from all sixteen counties of the state and beyond. In 2021, the MWPA held ninety-five writing conferences, workshops, and events in locations across Maine and online. To help make our programs accessible, MWPA offered nearly $30,000 in scholarships and fellowships to Maine writers at all stages of their careers last year.

About the Maine Chapbook Series

Between 1983 and 1999, thirteen chapbooks were published by the Maine Arts Commission in collaboration with a series of small Maine presses, and then by the Maine Writers & Publishers Alliance, as part of the Maine Chapbook Series. Each year, a nationally known writer served as the judge and selected a manuscript for publication. In 2019, the MWPA re-started this beloved series.

Previous Maine Chapbook Series Winners

Ruth Mendelson, *Sixteen Pastorals*
Theodore Press, 1983
Selected by Philip Booth

Rebecca Cummings, *Kaisa Kilponen*
Coyote Love Press, 1986
Selected by George Garrett

Robert Chute, *Samuel Sails for Home*
Coyote Love Press
Selected by Charles Simic

Christopher Fahy, *One Day in the Short Happy Life of Anna Banana*
Coastwise Press, 1988
Selected by Mary McCarthy

Kenneth Rosen, *The Hebrew Lion*
Ascensius Press, 1989
Selected by Amy Clampitt

Denis Ledoux, *Mountain Dance*
Coastwise Press, 1990
Selected by Elizabeth Hardwick

Besty Sholl, *Pick a Card*
Coyote/Bark Publications, 1991
Selected by Donald Hall

John A.S. Rogers, *The Elephant on the Tracks and Other Stories*
Muse Press, 1994
Selected by David Huddle

Candice Stover, *Holding Patterns*
Muse Press, 1994
Selected by Mary Oliver

Sis Deans, *Decisions and Other Stories*
Maine Writers & Publishers Alliance, 1995
Selected by Cathie Pelletier

Peter Harris, *Blue Hallelujahs*
Maine Writers & Publishers Alliance, 1996
Selected by Roland Flint

Rhea Cote Robbins, *Wednesday's Child*
Maine Writers & Publishers Alliance, 1997
Selected by Sven Birkerts

Ellen Bryan Obed, *A Letter from the Snow*
Maine Author's Publishing, 1999
Selected by Lois Lowry

Suzanne Langlois, *Bright Glint Gone*
Maine Writers & Publishers Alliance, 2020
Selected by Martha Collins

Brandon Dudley, *Hazards of Nature*
Maine Writers & Publishers Alliance, 2021
Selected by Sigrid Nunez

Coco McCracken, *The Rabbit*
Maine Writers & Publishers Alliance, 2022
Selected by Melissa Febos

About the Author

Born into a mixed-race family in Toronto, **Coco McCracken** has always been interested in writing about the intersectionality of place, race, and identity. With mystery shrouding her ancestry, her work is equal parts detective work and rhetorical relief, which comes from examining what it means to be a half-Asian, half-white woman, today. Now, raising a young daughter in Maine, she embarks on her new immigrant identity as half-Canadian, half-American. Coco currently has a newsletter called Coco's Echo, writes a monthly column for *Amjambo Africa*, and is working on her first full-length memoir.